HUMANITY CRIES

HUMANITY CRIES

SONDRA D. DAVIS

TATE PUBLISHING
AND ENTERPRISES, LLC

Published by Tate Publishing & Enterprises, LLC
127 E. Trade Center Terrace | Mustang, Oklahoma 73064 USA
1.888.361.9473 | www.tatepublishing.com

Tate Publishing is committed to excellence in the publishing industry. The company reflects the philosophy established by the founders, based on Psalm 68:11,
"The Lord gave the word and great was the company of those who published it."

Book design copyright © 2013 by Tate Publishing, LLC. All rights reserved.
Cover design by Joel Uber
Interior design by Jomel Pepito

Published in the United States of America

ISBN: 978-1-62746-630-1
1. Religion / Christian Life / General
13.09.05

CONTENTS

INTRODUCTION

A few years ago, astronomers reported that the earth was letting out a crying sound as it turns on its axis. I found this to be ironic because that is somewhat how I view the state of the world being before I heard the report. I see it in a state of distress that needs to be addressed and attended to immediately. There appears to be a growing number of people that are filled with dissatisfaction with their lives. They seem to have a constant hurt that lingers in their spirit. Unfortunately, until that hurt is released, those individuals will find ways to distribute that same hurt onto the lives of others.

Stopping this hurt is a task of God's people. We must first love God, truly love ourselves, and have love for our fellow man. This process can only begin with you taking action. The pages of this book are reminders that God has a life of abundance in store for all of us. He is the source of all that we will ever need in order to overcome the very challenges we face. There is nothing that shall by any means hinder the very promises that have been ordained over your life. God's people must rise up and realize that you are the only person that can stop yourself from obtaining everything God has to offer you. Believe in yourself and know that you are one of God's own creations. You are his seed, and you were planted in this earth for a purpose.

Use the words of this book to gain the insight that is needed in order for you to know and understand that you are predestined. Know that there is indeed a predetermination of your expected end, and it was established long before you came into existence. Now the set time has come. It is time for you to go, do, and become the destiny placed in you to be. Be bold and stand on the Word of God as your foundation. Take your place in bringing heaven to earth. Recognize that a change must take place in this world and that change must begin with you. Make a decree and declare that you will do the work that is necessary in order to make that change occur.

> If a man say, I love God, and hateth his brother, he is a liar: for he that loveth not his brother whom he hath seen, how can he love God whom he hath not seen? And this commandment have we from him, That he who loveth God love his brother also.
>
> 1 John 4:20–21

REALIZATION

In all these things we are more than conquerors through Him who loved us.

Romans 8:37 (KJV)

The first step to realization is to know that there is indeed something greater than ourselves inside us. It has nothing to do with the materialistic or physical attributes that the world often places on a pedestal. The world is waiting on you to bring forth the gifting that lies inside you.

Perhaps you have witnessed others delve into their "gift" and wonder when it will be your turn to experience the goodness that God seems to be handing out to others. The truth is that he is waiting on you to realize and move in the anointing that has been placed inside you. Even before the day of your existence, you were chosen to carry out a specific mission. That is what I call your assignment. No one can accomplish your assignment the way you can. It is your calling.

Once realization is attained, stepping out requires faith. It appears that going through life, one often expects for something to happen; has it ever occurred to you that you are that something waiting to happen? Many times, it may seem to be some sort of constant hindrance that holds us back from experiencing all the promises of God. Amazingly enough it is often ourselves that keeps us from our potential.

It is easier to claim someone else responsible for our own shortcomings. The absolute truth is that no one can hold us back from something that has been promised. The key to carrying out that promise is in knowing what we possess. Once we know who we are in God, it is impossible for us to be hindered or be held back by any outside forces. We have to know that there is greatness placed inside us. Once we know of that greatness, it is important for us to choose to move forward in it and never give up.

> Verily, verily, I say unto you, He that believeth on me, the works that I do shall he do also; and greater works than these shall he do; because I go unto my Father.
>
> John 14:12 (KJV)

There needs to be some point in life where we come to realize that we must step into our assignment and stand firm. The promises of God are already given to those of us who believe. It is evident that in order for us to truly understand the greatness that lies within us, we must first believe that it is indeed there. The more indecisive we are about having courage to walk in our gifting, the more likely we are to become stuck in a state of being paralyzed. We become afraid to move forward, fearing the unknown that lies ahead. This choice is made because it allows us to feel safe, comfortable, and secure. What sense does it make to stay stuck in a situation that we somehow know has no way of freeing us from the bondage of ourselves? We talk ourselves into thinking several reasons of why we cannot accomplish the very thing we are sent in this earth to do. Sometimes we give excuses such as being too old or that we are not the right person for the assignment. Who are we to dare not perceive ourselves to be fully equipped?

The moment we begin to question our capabilities is when we open the door to doubting our abilities. There must be a submission given by us to the very thing that God says lies within us. There can be no room for doubt. His Word is the seed that must be planted within us in order for us to reap the harvest that awaits us. There has to be a certainty that no matter what we think we are, we are the very person that God has ordained for the job.

> Being confident of this very thing, that he which hath begun a good work in you will perform it until the day of Jesus Christ.

Philippians 1:6 (KJV)

It takes confidence in order to realize that the assignment given to you was born with your name attached to it. Who you are needs to be looked upon as a proclamation of the magnitude of your existence, which is given to you and comes through you by God. The heart must be open as the mind is subjected to the realization of the "big" inside you. The greatness comes in knowing that all that is needed has already been provided. It must resonate strong within your spirit that nothing that comes against you is greater than that which lies within you.

> Ye are of God, little children, and have overcome them: because greater is he that is in you, than he that is in the world.

1 John 4:4 (KJV)

Take the necessary steps needed in order to move yourself forward in the direction that was predestined for you. God is waiting on you to answer the call. Remove doubt and replace it with certainty of who he has made you to be. Allow yourself to be released from guilt, shame, disbelief, and any other arbitrary thing that may have you bound. Wisdom comes in the knowing. Freedom comes in the doing. You can only do what you say and see yourself doing and becoming. If you say and see nothing, then that is what will occur. There is so much power that has been given to you. The breath of life was breathed in you to live to your fullest until you overflow. The abundance of his greatness is inside you. Realization that God is who he is and he could have gotten another to play your role; however, he chooses you, makes a bold statement about that greatness.

The lack of realizing our importance has caused so many people to miss the mark today. The way we see ourselves also determines how we view others. Judging ourselves and others, deeming there worth and value based on the world's way of thinking has created an imbalance. In the kingdom of God, we are all his children; and when we become born again in him, we all have access to everything that is his. The good news, the true gospel, is that it is all his, therefore it is yours.

> The earth is the Lord's, and the fullness thereof; the world, and they that dwell therein. Psalm 24:1 (KJV)

Once there is insight to this revelation, it must become prevalent in order for it to work. Have you heard the saying "the word will work, if you work it?" Find the verses in his Word that line up with the inadequacies you think you have and meditate on them. The meditation of the verses will help you to realize your greatness and also aid you in achieving victory over every circumstance. Possibilities are endless when there is a strong foundation in place that cannot be shaken.

LOVE

Thou shalt not avenge, nor bear any grudge against the children of thy people, but thou shalt love thy neighbor as thyself: I am the LORD.

Leviticus 19:18 (KJV)

Walk in love. Walking in love is the most important factor that we must practice. When we act on the very thing that we were actually produced out of, our potential is endless. God has given us the ability to show how much we trust in his love for us. Treating each other the way we want to be treated at all times is an indication of our awareness of his love for us. Recognition of this action provides us with an open door to his grace, mercy, and goodness, which gives light to the spirit that feeds the soul.

There has to be a constant effort made on a daily basis to not allow the outside world to penetrate the inner core of who you are. I have grown to realize that it is me who determines my inner temperature and to what degree I will let it rise and/or fall. If allowed, people will take you outside of the best part of who you are; and you will not even know how you ended up there.

The manner that love comes to you is determined by the way that you give and receive it. Your walk is what determines your path. The love of God is infinite. This infinite love of God has the ability to fill you up and make you whole. It is our obedience, surrendering to his will, and trusting in his Word that shows our love for him.

We must first love God as well as love ourself. It is impossible to give away what you do not possess inside yourself. Simply put, this means, how is it possible for you to love your neighbor if there are things you do not love about yourself? When there is no clear realization of the love God has for you, it is impossible for you to reach outside of yourself and love others.

Love is the solution that will enable us to reach a more in-depth level of thinking, acting, and being. The practice of love in how we walk, how we talk, how we act, and how we are is what will open the gates of opportunity. The moment we choose to not love, we have made the choice to place limitations on what we receive.

Ultimately, it is love that keeps us connected. How we handle a situation determines whether or not we know the true meaning of the "love walk." His love is not conditional. It is not based or measured according to what we feel emotionally. God is love; therefore everything he is, is love. That love is the example of how we are to be.

Let brotherly love continue.

Hebrews 13:1 (KJV)

You are formed out of the love of God. View each day as a new opportunity to give someone more love than you did the day before. Start with yourself, and then let it exude outward to reach as many as you can. Love is the key that will break down the disillusionment that has caused pain to so many people. The lack of love in this earth has caused destruction of the mind, body, and spirit. Being an example of the love that God is to you can change the very essence of this world.

The world will only rise to the level of love in which we place within it. People are in need of healing in their mind, heart, and spirit. Everyday people cry out to be acknowledged and cared for—loved. It is the responsibility of God's people to adhere to that cry. There is only one thing that can silence that cry and that is love. Having blinded eyes to what is clearly in front of us can no longer be the solution. Love is what is needed in order to effectively change this earth into what God determined it to be. The truth of love is to know what it truly is; and more importantly, how to be able to give, share, receive, and be it to others. Your blessing comes so that you may be a blessing to someone else. Allowing someone else to partake of your love should not only feed your spirit but also open your eyes, mind, and heart. The pulse of who God is can only permeate in this earth if we as a people determine the wealth of love that it will take to change it. As long as we view the well-being of another individual as outside of ourselves, there cannot be change.

> The liberal soul shall be made fat: and he that watereth shall be watered also himself.
>
> Proverbs 11:25 (KJV)

Oftentimes, it is viewed that as long as something does not affect the outcome of us making it to where our destination is, then it does not matter. This cycle is a curse that must be stopped. There has to be a deeper love for all mankind. True revelation about the love of God and the heart that has been placed inside us to have for one another's well-being must be learned and then exercised. We have to treat one another as if each individual is an extension of ourselves.

> This is my commandment that ye love one another, as I have loved you.
>
> John 15:12 (KJV)

There are many steps that can be taken to start the love process. First, we have to renew our mind. This comes by reading and meditating the Word of God. Second, we must take action and be willing to let our flesh die daily. Third, we must look pass the senses of being offended. We cannot allow our emotions to control us. Finally, we must take victory over each situation and realize the most effective way to handle them is with love. We must remind ourselves of the love that it took for Christ to die for our sins. It is the same type of love that we must have for our fellow man. It is indeed by grace that we all are saved. Looking at someone and determining that what they encounter is not our problem is not the way this world was intended to be. The heart of God went beyond what was his son and reached out to all people. He sacrificed his son so that we have an opportunity to live.

The ways of this world are wicked; however, it does not give free reign for us to be that way. As children of the Most High God, we are the ones that have the ability to change this world and make it what he intended it to be. We must learn how to love. Open your heart so wide that it will be impossible for any corruption to uproot the good seed that has been planted. Let no man place upon your heart anything outside of what the Word of God speaks. There can be no wavering. Do what you do for God, and you shall experience the promises that he has made unto you. The opinions or ways of other people should not determine your behavior. We are to act out God's own heart—giving, doing, and being what God has written. Your actions must not be done for the approval or recognition of others. You must remember your purpose. If someone does not respond the way you want them to, check your agenda. Why were you doing what you did? Was it out of love? If the answer is yes, then there is no fixed outcome of how the other individual should react.

Let your love be unconditional. Respect and set boundaries for yourself. Let your love flow bountifully so that God can bless you in the same manner. Do what you do to the glorification of what God has done and is doing for you. The example of love that you provide for others, God will always reciprocate back to you.

> Beloved, let us love one another: for love is of God; and every one that loveth is born of God, and knoweth God. He that loveth not knoweth not God; for God is love.
>
> 1 John 4:7-8 (KJV)

PIE MENTALITY

My God shall supply all your need according to His
riches in glory by Christ Jesus.

Philippians 4:19 (KJV)

I remember a time when it seemed that people opened their
hearts wider and were more willing to help one another.
This is the type of action that assisted people in moving into
their particular position of purpose. There seemed to be a
time where more people seemed to come together to create
change. Now it seems more common for each individual
to look out for themselves. People of today appear to care
less when it comes to the well-being of others. This type of
behavior has to change. We can only make a true impact if
the people of God come together for a common purpose.
That purpose must be centered and grounded in love. We
must realize that we have a responsibility to do our part in
changing the very world that we live in. There appears to be

a growing misconception that if someone gets theirs, then there will be less or none for the next person. Oftentimes, this creates an internal battle that can influence one to believe that one person gaining means another person losing. This is not the truth according to the Word of God.

> Delight thyself also in the LORD; and he shall give thee the desires of thine heart.

> Psalms 37:4 (KJV)

There is no shortage in the kingdom. He is the provider and creator of all. There is absolutely nothing that is withheld from those that know and reverence who God is. The way God revealed it to me is so simple, and I will share it with you. The revelation came to me in my spirit using pie. I know that may sound strange but just read on. I was reminded that every pie has its own name like apple, cherry, strawberry, lemon, etc. It came to me that we as his children have our own pie. The pie never runs out. Once we partake from the pie, which can be viewed as our gifts, anointing, and/or success, it is replenished. Let me be clear, no one can eat up your pie. They may indulge in what is yours by tasting it through the works that you do; however, you are the only one who can truly determine the portion they receive. It is up to you, so choose wisely who you decide to invite to your table.

> And God is able to make all grace abound toward
> you; that ye, always having all sufficiency in all
> things, may abound to every good work:

2 Corinthians 9:8 (kjv)

The next pie revelation came to me this way; eating it is an action of movement. The pie does not jump into your mouth; it requires action on your part to get it there. Cutting in to or tasting pie does not always reveal the ingredients that it maintains. You won't know what you have inside you if you spend all of your time guessing. Use the utensils that God has provided and dig in. Start with the Word, chew on it, savor it, and then swallow it. Let it digest in your spirit and rest in your heart.

It is in God that we ought to breathe, live, and have our being. You must move in accordance to what God speaks and places upon your heart. Always ask and seek God for his guidance. This will help to alleviate the actions that sometimes are taken that may not be what God has ordained for us to do. Oftentimes, these actions may appear that they are what need to be done in order to get ahead or create the solution "we" see fit for the circumstance. The only issue here is that we may not have the full picture of what is actually transpiring. This is why it is important that we do not allow whatever is going on to cause us to waver from what we know is placed in us to do. We should not be moved by our emotions or what we see in front of us. The Word of God is the truth of what we can have in our lives.

Wrapping our thoughts around the limitation of people and what they say and think will only lead to self-destruction. We must remember his benefits daily and make constant efforts to stay focused on what the Word of God says is available to us as his children. The longer we view God's blessings as being allotted in a certain amount, there is no clear truth for us of the realism of who God truly is.

> Blessed be the Lord, who daily loadeth us with benefits, even the God of our salvation. Selah.
>
> Psalms 68:19 (KJV)

When you truly know what is yours and the rights you have to it, sharing the goodness of what is inside you will not be fearful to you. We must have true revelation in the Word of God, which clearly states that we are one with him. Our Father is the Most High God. Our divine connection to God has given us the power to walk and have dominion in this earth. This type of thinking must be meditated. Meditation helps to change the ideal and thought pattern of the mind-set on shortage. God has placed us here to rule and have authority. It is up to us to take dominion.

> Let us not therefore judge one another anymore: but judge this rather, that no man put a stumblingblock or an occasion to fall in his brother's way.
>
> Romans 14:13 (KJV)

There is no need to try and trip somebody up or stop them from achieving. The more we focus on the achievements of others the world misses out on the gifts that abide within ourselves. We must replace the pie mentality with the kingdom mentality. A kingdom mentality is one that knows there is more than enough for all of us. The beauty is that the more we give with the heart of God, the more we will receive. All things will reciprocate, not just those that are concrete. The same giving action can be done with love and thoughts. How we see ourselves is how others will view us. If we see ourselves as the royalty that we are, then the mere idea of us running out of anything is dismissed. Royalty decrees and it is established. It must resonate in your spirit that you are royalty. Power is promised to you; and therefore, the outcome is determined—you win! We already have everything that we need. It is up to us to determine the level in which we will believe and act upon his Word. There is more than enough to do and be whatever God promised—that is kingdom mentality.

> Give, and it shall be given unto you; good measure, pressed down, and shaken together, and running over, shall men give into your bosom. For with the same measure that ye mete withal it shall be measured to you again.
>
> Luke 6:38 (KJV)

ASSOCIATION

A wise man will hear, and will increase learning; and a man of understanding shall attain unto wise counsels:

Proverbs 1:5 (KJV)

Who you position yourself around does indeed play a significant role in the outcome of your ability to soar. The meaning of this statement is simple. If you surround yourself with people who do not believe in flying there is a possibility that you too may stay grounded. The weight of constant battling may indeed affect not only your altitude but also your determination and destination.

Iron sharpeneth iron, so a man sharpeneth the countenance of his friend.

Proverbs 27:17 (KJV)

I cannot emphasize enough to stay rooted and grounded in the Word of God. The power of corrupt communication has the potential to enable you from having clear insight to the promises of God. This can cause many disruptions and detours to the plan that has already been established. One bad apple can indeed destroy the bunch. For example, if you constantly surround yourself with negative energy, then your positive energy will be affected. The constant pulling of your energies, by staying in a relationship or situation that does not feed your spirit or line up with what the Word speaks, can indeed uproot some planted seed. That is why you must sow where the ground is good.

There is a definite plot of the enemy to come for the Word that is planted inside you. When you receive the Word of God that is fed to you, it can be regurgitated out of you if it has not been digested properly. The constant encountering of negative energy can alter your speech, thoughts, and actions. It is imperative that you choose your alliances and those you associate with wisely. The Bible tells of many occasions where people's circumstances were attached to, altered, or changed by other people. For example, look at the relationship between Adam and Eve, Cain and Abel, Samson and Delilah. It is important that the people we choose to connect ourselves to and know also reverence God. We must know that God is the one that will provide us with everything we need.

I have learned that talking or confiding with someone outside of who God has said, always caused me confusion. As it states in the Word, confusion is not of God. Ask yourself important questions; they will help you to make the best choices regarding answers dealing with association. First of all, did I seek God? Who am I taking my direction and instructions from? Does the direction and instruction spoken to me aligned with what God has told me about myself and the situation? Have I truly considered what God has to say about what is going on with me? There must be a conscious effort to keep ourselves surrounded with people who understand and know that there is something greater than that of ourselves.

The truth of God makes us free. Seeking anything outside of that will keep us bound. In my years of living, I too have found myself asking others what they think about a certain situation I am going through. It was not until I grew wiser that I realized before talking to anyone, I have to have a talk with God. No one understands me or knows what is best for me like God does.

How we maneuver through this life and the way we do it makes a difference to the makeup of how we view ourselves and our possibilities. We are supposed to be walking representatives of the kingdom of God. Therefore, it is imperative that we monitor the degree to which we allow ourselves to be subjected to the world and its values. God takes the dealings we have with individuals and have them fit into the design he has for us. When we do not monitor our relationships, it has the potential to dispel our thoughts and change the very being of our soul.

> Give not that which is holy unto the dogs, neither cast ye your pearls before swine, lest they trample them under their feet, and turn again and rend you.
>
> Matthew 7:6 (KJV)

It does indeed matter who you share your vision, wisdom, and space with in this earth. The ability to transcend beyond what we see is directly connected to the truth of knowing who we are. A relationship that is Godly will recognize your greatness, challenge you, encourage you, and also enhance you to become all that you are meant to be. Therefore, it is essential that you constantly thrive to reach beyond the point of where you are. Make sure you surround yourself with dreamers who are achievers and believers that know and act upon God's word of "all things are possible." Another individual's thoughts, actions, and words can damage your crop. You must protect your harvest by guarding your heart. The early stages of your vision, all the way to its birth, are very precious and delicate; therefore, be mindful sharing it with someone who may not have the ability to handle it. Develop relationships that keep you in a state of being, doing, and moving forward.

Always pray and ask God for guidance and wisdom when choosing who needs to be a part of your life.

Oftentimes, it is unclear how long of a season certain people are to be in our lives. As people of God, we need to be mindful of our relationships. The key thing is that we must trust what God is doing in our lives and know that each individual serves a purpose. Our job is to learn the lessons they provide for our life at the moment they are in it. We must remember whether it is for a moment, a season, or a lifetime; God knows what is best for us.

ILLUSION

Love not the world, neither the things that are in the world. If any man love the world, the love of the Father is not in him.

For all that is in the world, the lust of the flesh, and the lust of the eyes, and the pride of life, is not of the Father, but is of the world.

And the world passeth away, and the lust thereof: but he that doeth the will of God abideth forever.

1 John 2:15-17 (KJV)

Contrary to the belief that what you see is always what you get, we live in a society where people constantly pretend to be something that they are not. People put on many different faces in hopes that no one will get to see the real person on the inside. When was the last time you really asked someone how they were doing? Do you think they told you the truth? A lot of times people are afraid to show who they are and what is really going on inside of them. They do not want to seem as if anything is penetrating them when in actuality it just may be consuming them.

I have found that smiles often adorn faces that hide saddened hearts and misguided spirits. People are lost and searching for truth and yet not willing to admit they are seeking it. It saddens me to think how much emphasis is placed on worldly possessions. There are too many people thinking that the measure of a man is determined by how much he is worth monetarily. The truth is that wealth is more than just money and how much we possess. It is a wholeness word that deals with being in a state of completeness. The more a person functions inside of the falsehood that is perpetrated within the world, the further they move away from God. It is necessary to take inventory of what we have going on inside of us so that we can become more in tune with the truth of our dominion. As people of God, we must be real and true and allow that realism to be the evidence of our existence. It has always baffled me when I see an individual who creates a facade in order to be perceived a certain way. They ride around in a car they cannot afford, dress in the finest of clothes they maxed out their credit cards to have, and yet they don't "own" anything. They do these things because they think it sets them within a class of people that have arrived. The funny thing is, where on earth have they arrived too? The strange thing is that this kind of behavior is glorified and has somewhat become common. A high-paying job, living in a huge home, driving a fancy car, and dressing well is often equated to being successful. The truth is that an individual cannot be measured by the things that they acquire. Determining the value of one's self comes when an individual knows their true self-worth in God.

The natural eye sees things as being one way and in actuality they are not. There are several people walking around with their eyes wide shut. Going through the mundane routines of life and not being involved for one minute. They appear to be engaged with life and yet really have no connection to it. They walk around looking without truly seeing, being, and yet not really doing anything. Their actions may just be for show in hopes that whoever is observing them will not catch a glimpse of who they truly are. It is my belief that at some point, in order for things to change, there has to be an epiphany with God's people. We must realize it is not how blessed we are that makes us, but it is how much of a blessing we can be to those around us. No longer should it be acceptable to hide behind what someone else's standards of living are. Be true to who you are. Make a statement with your words and actions. Get beyond what you drive and what you wear.

> For what is a man advantaged, if he gain the whole world, and lose himself, or be cast away?
>
> Luke 9:25 (KJV)

What good is it to have things, and yet there is an emptiness that is lurking inside you. Time and time again, I have noticed that the very thing that is harnessed within the spirit is produced in our lives. Money cannot buy happiness, don't get me wrong I am fully aware that it is something needed in order to operate effectively in this world. Think about some of those who do have a lot of money such as celebrities or other prominent people in the public eye, they are viewed as "having it all." What is your definition of "all?" All is another wholeness word that circumferences everything. "All" is something that needs to be determined from the inside out. I recognize that being considered as looking a certain way or doing certain things as mentioned above is what often gets results; but, how real is that? You have to ask yourself, are we allowing standards to be set by people who themselves may not know the truth? Have you ever contemplated the notion that they too are walking blindly? Have you ever thought that the very people you envy may not be satisfied with themselves? Could they possibly be living their lives according to what someone else believes?

> Let them alone: they be blind leaders of the blind. And if the blind lead the blind, both shall fall into the ditch.
>
> Matthew 15:14 (KJV)

Living life for God fully is the best way to ensure that you have the clear vision of God. What is meant by this is that, God sets the standards. Allow God to create in you the level that decides what true victory is. The envisioning of the truth is what must determine the outcome of reality. The state of the world is as bleak as the vision. Seeking the approval of others will only bring disappointment. We must realize that society is merely a structure that we play a huge role in creating. If there is no movement of action toward a better society then one will never occur.

We must see ourselves moving, doing, and being better individuals. Ask for the guidance of God and take the time to figure out what a great world would look like. Determine your role, and then make sure it is in alignment with God's vision. Once that is done, see it and create it in your mind. Speak it with your words. Take the necessary steps to make it happen. I know this perspective changed my life. I made a vow to do my best to keep my word and be exactly who I claim to be. Whoever I say that I am when someone is watching is the same one I am when no one is there. This decision has really made me become a more productive person with greater integrity.

MIND CONTROL

For as he thinketh in his heart, so is he: Eat and drink, saith he to thee; but his heart is not with thee.

Proverbs 23:7 (KJV)

What do you think about yourself? Do you think that you are worthy of all that God has done for you? Do you think you have done what God has placed you in this world to do? Do you think that you make a difference? Do you think you can do anything to change the state that you are in right now? Do you think that you have the power to change the state of someone else? Do you see yourself achieving? What do you think are the thoughts that God thinks toward you?

As I stated before, the way we think has a lot to do with the way we live our lives. Therefore, the thoughts we ponder the most shows up in the life we create for ourselves. Just as positive thinking can create something good for us, negative thinking can produce just the opposite. Whatever we have sown in our heart is what manifests. Our thoughts have to stay focused on the vision that God has placed on the inside of us. Negative thoughts have the potential to cloud the mind, which may eventually consume all that is within us. God's plan for our life is prosperity. The Word of God speaks volumes to the measure in which God wants us to achieve. The more we get our thoughts clear of conflicting opinions to what is spoken in the Word of God, the more apt we are to know our place in him.

I have found the truth to be that whatever we think about ourselves is often the way others will perceive us. If we think ourselves unworthy, then we will conduct certain behaviors that will line up with that thinking, thereby producing certain actions. The actions produce a certain result. The result then dictates back to us the very thought which then has the tendency to assure what we were thinking was correct. It becomes a cycle that can only be broken by changing our thought pattern.

> For God hath not given us the spirit of fear; but of power, and of love, and of a sound mind.
>
> 2 Timothy 1:7 (KJV)

Every day we must order our day by making sure that our thoughts about ourselves are in alignment with that of the Word of God. Sometimes it may appear difficult; however, it is important that we take inventory of how we think. That may sound strange; however, it is the first step to really seeing what type of energy we are calling forth into our lives. For example, how do you find yourself looking at situations? Thinking in a positive manner about circumstances and situations that occur in your life is a choice that must be made daily. I have found that one of the best ways to do this is first thing in the morning. This allows you to start your day set in the right frame of mind.

> And be not conformed to this world: but be ye transformed by the renewing of your mind, that ye may prove what is that good, and acceptable, and perfect, will of God.

Romans 12:2 (KJV)

The right frame of mind begins with a process that is known as renewal of the mind. The only way to renew your mind is to make sure that you have girded yourself up with the Word of God. This will help build your spirit, which in turn will aid you in getting your thoughts under submission to the right way of thinking. It may seem difficult at first; however, it is the only way that I found to work for me. Every day I start by thanking God for loving me. It allows me to center the rest of my thoughts on that—love. I cannot tell God thank you for loving me without reminding myself of the love he has for me.

I have had several occasions where I thought myself out of something that could have possibly been great for me. I let my thoughts get the best of me and allowed it to ultimately stop me from doing what I needed to do. We must allow our mind to wrap itself around the idea that God is God. He has placed so much greatness inside us. It is up to us to stay connected to him. Our thinking must stay in a state of peace. That place of peace is one of rest. Allowing our mind to rest upon what God thinks about us will open many doorways to seeing clearly. The heart has to grab hold of God's vision, and then our mind must come into agreement with it. It is the mind and the thoughts that we perceive that become our reality. Thoughts can make you move or keep you stagnant. The thoughts we place in our mind are what play a vital role in telling us whether or not we will move forth in our calling. Remember that the world is waiting on you to do the part in which God has called you to do. Knowing the Word of God for yourself will grant you access to the wisdom that you need in order to move forth in your calling.

Negative thinking has the ability to warp our speech and trap our words. This is a serious issue, which I will discuss in the next chapter. It is very important that negative thoughts are replaced with positive ones. This method will head you in the right direction that will allow God to have his way. Now ask yourself, do I have the power to change my life? My answer to you is, of course you do. Just remember to start by changing the way you think. The faster you think you can, the quicker you will believe you can. Once you believe you can, then you will know you can. Knowing is the key to what is needed to propel you into action.

WORD SUPREMACY

Death and life are in the power of the tongue: and
they that love it shall eat the fruit thereof.

Proverbs 18:21 (KJV)

A re you using your words to bless or curse those around
you? Do you choose your words wisely? Words are very
powerful. They have the ability to command, create, and
bring into existence your thoughts. You must realize that
what you say is what you will have. We must also recognize
that the words spoken out of our mouths are declarations.
These words are the very things that put things into action.
As I mentioned in the last chapter, this is why it is very
important that we think before we speak.

The heart of the wise teacheth his mouth, and
addeth learning to his lips.

Proverbs 16:23 (KJV)

The words that we speak have two possibilities. They have the power to construct or destruct. As a child of God, it is important that we use our words to build and restore others. The way that we use words have the ability to change a person's life forever. Every time you encounter another individual, the words you speak must be chosen wisely. There is a popular statement that goes "sticks and stones may break my bones but names won't ever hurt me." This is a false statement. Verbal abuse is just as damaging as physical abuse. When there is physical abuse there is a visible bruise that often appears. Unlike verbal abuse, during physical abuse, we can see the wound or mark that was made and witness the healing process it takes to repair it. I understand the fact that physical abuse goes deeper than my brief explanation; but in this instance, I want to focus on the potential of damaging words.

> Whoso keepeth his mouth and his tongue keepeth his soul from troubles.
>
> Proverbs 21:23 (KJV)

The words that you say to someone may stay with them for the rest of their lives. The words can become embedded in their mind and effect the very countenance of their spirit. This can hurt them immediately and/or linger on with them for a lengthy period of time. They may rehearse the words over and over and allow them to cause all types of psychological problems such as low self-esteem, insecurity, doubt, and even self-hatred. Therefore, we must always remember to choose our words wisely because of the power they possess.

> A brother offended is harder to be won than a strong city: and their contentions are like the bars of a castle.

> Proverbs 18:19 (KJV)

Not only is what we say important, but how it is said makes a difference. The way the words are spoken and how you use your words will determine how they may be perceived. Check yourself even before you open your mouth. Think about how the words you speak may affect the person. Will you be adding to who they are or taking away from who they are on their way to becoming? When you are speaking to them, will your words be healing to their spirit or be rotten to their bones? One of the simplest ways to examine your words potentiality is asking yourself, "Is what I am about to say something I would like to be said to myself?" Was time taken to think about what you want to say or what you are going to say? Did you just speak without even thinking about how it may affect the other person? Time is up for excuses. We have to take responsibility for our words just as we do our actions. Speaking to someone boorishly and blaming them for our responses such as saying things like, "I had to get that person straight and give them a piece of my mind" or perhaps something like

"They needed to be told a thing or two," do not warrant any manner of justification.

> Speak not evil one of another, brethren. He that speaketh evil of his brother, and judgeth his brother, speaketh evil of the law, and judgeth the law: but if thou judge the law, thou art not a doer of the law, but a judge.

> James 4:11 (KJV)

There is another aspect on the power of words that I must mention. I believe it has become so common that it is overlooked upon as being sinful. Gossip is an abomination to God. God is not pleased when his people gossip or tear down one another. Whether the individual we are talking about is absent of the discussion of what is being spoken, does not matter because the ultimate listener and judge is present— God. Everything is known unto him; and therefore, it is in our best interest to make sure we guard the words of our mouth. We must know when to use it as a tool and when to keep it bridled. How can you tell if what you are doing is gossip? It is simple. If the individual is not present and you are talking about them, speaking against them or their situation, it is gossip. I too have had to repent when realizing the seriousness of God's perception of gossip. It is an abomination (Prov. 6:16–19, KJV). The best and only way according to the Word of God to deal with someone is to go to that person directly (Matt. 18:15–17, KJV).

But I say unto you, That every idle word that men shall speak, they shall give account thereof in the day of judgment.

Matthew 12:36 (KJV)

God gave us the ability to speak, because he knew the power that words possess. Look in the Bible and see how many times God used words to do his work. It is the word of God that still speaks today. The Word of God has power and can be used to teach, love, create, heal, cleanse, guide, instruct, perfect, counsel, and the list goes on. The same elements of power are given to us. We possess the power of speaking things into being; therefore, take heed to what you speak and always do your best to use your words wisely.

Let no corrupt communication proceed out of your mouth, but that which is good to the use of edifying, that it may minister grace unto the hearers.

Let all bitterness, and wrath, and anger, and clamor, and evil speaking, be put away from you, with all malice: And be ye kind one to another, tenderhearted, forgiving one another, even as God for Christ's sake hath forgiven you.

Ephesians 4:29,31–32 (KJV)

RESPONSIBLE ACCOUNTABILITY

Ye are the salt of the earth: but if the salt have lost his savour, wherewith shall it be salted? it is thenceforth good for nothing, but to be cast out, and to be trodden under foot of men.

Ye are the light of the world. A city that is set on an hill cannot be hid.

Neither do men light a candle, and put it under a bushel, but on a candlestick; and it giveth light unto all that are in the house.

Let your light so shine before men, that they may see your good works, and glorify your Father which is in heaven.

Matthew 5:13–16 (KJV)

The Word of God tells us who we are and what we need to do. As his people, we have been given dominion over this earth. For that reason, it's impertinent that we grab hold of this revelation and realize that we are the light of this world. It is therefore our responsibility to rise up and give light to all that are within this earth. We must allow the love of God to work through us, because we are the ones who will recover the lost. It is up to us to let them know that they are not forgotten. We must engulf them with the same love that we experienced when we came into being one with God.

Being a part of the glorious light of God means you have the capability to cast out darkness. The purpose of that light is to therefore shine. That light must shine with an authority that commands all darkness to flee. There should be evidence of the encounter we have had with God. As children of God, we must take ownership over what happens to our brothers and sisters here on earth.

So I ask you, "Are you your brother's keeper?" After reading the pages of this book, your answer is hopefully emphatically resonating within your inner core, that yes you are. All of mankind is your kind. It is up to you to make a difference in this world. If you agree that there is definitely work that needs to be done, then take your place in the solution of the situation and do something about it. The world is rapidly changing, and it seems that the hearts of the majority of people are changing with it.

There appears to be a growing contingency for individuals to only look out for themselves. People are moving at such a fast pace that very seldom do they take the time to check and see how the next person is doing. Temperaments have become shorter than they used to be. The patience, love, compassion, and consideration that used to be prevalent seem to have become a rarity.

We have to take responsibility and say to ourselves what is it that I can do to help my fellow man. Energy and time are often wasted because of blaming and/or pointing fingers at the next individual and saying what they can do. Taking responsibility means right there in the moment making ourselves accountable and doing something to create the change that is needed. It is time that we look at the role we play in the current state of the world's people. If there is no willingness of God's people to stand up and take responsibility for the condition of the people in this world, then they will not progress any further than their current circumstances.

> For I was an hungred, and ye gave me no meat: I was thirsty, and ye gave me no drink:
>
> I was a stranger, and ye took me not in: naked, and ye clothed me not: sick, and in prison, and ye visited me not. Then shall they also answer him, saying, Lord, when saw we thee an hungred, or athirst, or a stranger, or naked, or sick, or in prison, and did not minister unto thee?

Then shall he answer them, saying, Verily I say unto you, Inasmuch as ye did it not to one of the least of these, ye did it not to me.

And these shall go away into everlasting punishment: but the righteous into life eternal.

Matthew 25:42–46 (KJV)

This passage from the Bible leaves no question on what God expects to transpire from within our hearts all the way out to the works of our hands. It informs us of the level of magnitude that is looked upon when it comes to loving one another. The love we have for each other has to go beyond just recognizing needs. There is an obligation to do what it takes to make sure those needs are met. There is no excuse for these conditions great enough to surpass anything that can be imaginable. It is impossible to conquer the situation if it continuously is ignored.

People are dying every day from destitute conditions. They are afflicted and in desperate need of the healing that only God can provide. God has given this world to us; therefore, it is our territory. Nothing in this earth can be done if we do not acknowledge, confront, and deal with the situation. The longer excuses are made, the more people will remain in a state of confusion. Do not allow one more moment of your life to pass you by and not recognize the important call God has placed on you within humanity. The charge he gave is the one that will save the lives of those in need. Responding to the cause of rectifying and restoring the people of this earth the way God intended can only take place with us taking action. Ask God for guidance. Listen for his instruction. Hear and obey what is spoken to your spirit. This will determine what you need to do and the direction you need to take.

ACTIVE AUTHORITY

If a brother or sister be naked, and destitute of daily food, And one of you say unto them, Depart in peace, be ye warmed and filled; notwithstanding ye give them not those things which are needful to the body; what doth it profit?

Even so faith, if it hath not works, is dead, being alone.

Yea, a man may say, Thou hast faith, and I have works: shew me thy faith without thy works, and I will shew thee my faith by my works.

But wilt thou know, O vain man, that faith without works is dead?

James 2:15–18, 20 (KJV)

It is time to take a stand, make a difference, and do something. God placed you here to do his work in this earth. You are a significant part of the solution to the problems that are in this world. Each one of us has a specific task that must be accomplished. Start off by looking at yourself and determine what you can do in order to make a difference. I know that the quick answer may be, "I am going to pray and hope things change." Prayer does indeed change things; however, along with that prayer we must be willing to roll up our sleeves and get busy. The people of God must reach out and mend the broken hearts and heal the wounded spirits. We must stop wasting time and get to work.

> He also that is slothful in his work is brother to him that is a great waster.
>
> Proverbs 18:9 (KJV)

There is indeed a lot of work that needs to be done. We cannot allow this to overwhelm us. One of the ways to begin the journey of change is to find out which cause makes you the most passionate. Is it the homeless man on the street? Find a way to get him shelter. Is it the woman who cannot feed her family? Determine how you can help her get some food to feed her family. Is it the child who does not respect his/her elders? Spend time with that child and help them learn the value and wisdom of the elderly. Perhaps your cause is the child who cannot read. Take the time to volunteer and teach them to read. Are you angered by the way your neighborhood is changing? Maybe it's time you start a neighborhood watch. There is a lot of work that needs to be done, and we have everything we need right here to do it. We are the body of Christ, and it is in him that we need to move. It is the love of your heart along with the work of your hands that will create newness in this earth. Right now is the time that we must use what God gave us in order to get the job done.

> When the righteous are in authority, the people rejoice: but when the wicked beareth rule, the people mourn.
>
> Proverbs 29:2 (KJV)

We have the nature of God within us; and therefore must rise up with authority to take back what rightfully is given to us. We must take charge. We have to claim the lost, and let them continuously know that God loves them and that we love them. We have the capability to show them, through our works, what love is; and it must be done without fail. It is our duty to do the necessary work. This is the only way to build the kingdom of God. We have to make the choice to take action. Until we do the task, it will remain incomplete. What we do as his people makes a statement to others about who God is. Until some people grow beyond what it is they think they know, you may very well be the only Bible they read. It is, therefore, very important that you realize it is not just the words you speak but also the works that you do that speaks the greatest multitudes about you.

> For God is not unrighteous to forget your work and labour of love, which ye have shewed toward his name, in that ye have ministered to the saints, and do minister.
>
> Hebrews 6:10 (KJV)

CONCLUSION

Commit thy works unto the Lord, and thy thoughts shall be established.

Proverbs 16:3 (KJV)

You may be thinking and asking yourself what I can do to make a difference. It must begin with a transformation taking place within you. Reading the Word of God and obeying what it says will speak to your heart exactly what you need to do. The Bible has principles that give specifications of what God expects, who he is, and the power he possesses. It provides instructions for you on how to do what is needed.

Realize that God has created you with the same power that is within him. Be aware of that power, and do not lose sight of what you are to accomplish in this earth. Create within yourself a solid foundation of love for all people. This love will move you to do things you never dreamt possible to do. It will help you to love your enemies and help your fellow man without expectation of receiving anything in return. Newness will form in your heart once you learn and truly grasp that someone else's needs are indeed in some way a part of your own.

Know that there is no shortage in this earth, that thinking is only in the state of our intellectual mentality. This type of thinking is not kingdom based. God has provided and will continue to provide more than enough for all of his children. It is up to us to do something about the world's current state. Ask God for guidance. Be mindful of your associations, as well as those you choose to have speak into your life. Surround yourself with individuals that are positive, like-minded, and equally yoked. Your relationships do indeed have an impact on your state of mind and spirit.

This type of awareness will help you to make certain that you do not allow yourself to be caught up in any illusions that can alter your direction. Be diligent in your pursuit of keeping your mind focused on what God speaks to you. This will assist you with keeping your thoughts and words in alignment with that of God. Start taking heed to his Word and acting on it. Remember that we have to take ownership. It is our responsibility to attend to our Father's business, which are his people. He gave us authority, and now it is up to us to use it. Become the change you want to see; and do so by doing it, living it, and being it. These types of actions will provide the example of what this world can be—a better place not just for some, but for all. Are we our brother's keeper? My answer is yes we are.

> For the body is not one member, but many. If the foot shall say, Because I am not the hand, I am not of the body; is it therefore not of the body?

> And if the ear shall say, Because I am not the eye, I am not of the body; is it therefore not of the body?

> If the whole body were an eye, where were the hearing? If the whole were hearing, where were the smelling? But now hath God set the members every one of them in the body, as it hath pleased him.

> And if they were all one member, where were the body? But now are they many members, yet but one body.

> And the eye cannot say unto the hand, I have no need of thee: nor again the head to the feet, I have no need of you. Nay, much more those members of the body, which seem to be more feeble, are necessary: And those members of the body, which we think to be less honourable, upon these we bestow more abundant honour; and our uncomely parts have more abundant comeliness.

> For our comely parts have no need: but God hath tempered the body together, having given more abundant honour to that part which lacked:

That there should be no schism in the body; but that the members should have the same care one for another.

And whether one member suffer, all the members suffer with it; or one member be honoured, all the members rejoice with it.

Now ye are the body of Christ, and members in particular.

1 Corinthians 12:14–27 (KJV)